Then & Now
NASHUA

On May 24, 1688, orders from England made clear to the pioneers of the Massachusetts Bay Colony township of Dunstable, "the selectman are to lay out the Kings hyway, throu the Town to Nashawa river, and lay out Convenient hyway frome the generall hy (way) to merimathe River, where it may be best and do lest damag to the lot whear it must ly through." Almost 200 years later, in 1886, the year of this map, the forest of Dunstable has been transformed into a busy industrialized city with the Kings Highway as the Main Street served by Canal Street, the original convenient highway created to reach the Merrimack River. Horsecars on rail lines were just newly in place in 1886, creating an even greater affair of activity. Mass transit made traveling in the city for trade, commerce, and communication a new convenience instead of a challenging hardship. (Courtesy Library of Congress.)

THEN & NOW

NASHUA

Robin Ann Peters

ARCADIA

Published by Arcadia Publishing
Charleston SC, Chicago IL, Portsmouth NH, San Francisco CA

Printed in the United States of America

Library of Congress Catalog Card Number: 2005931902

For all general information contact Arcadia Publishing at:
Telephone 843-853-2070
Fax 843-853-0044
E-mail sales@arcadiapublishing.com
For customer service and orders:
Toll-Free 1-888-313-2665

Visit us on the internet at http://www.arcadiapublishing.com

*With loving memory to my godmother, Suzanne Rita Francoeur, who lived
and loved with us from January 18, 1944 until May 3, 2004.
A portion of the earnings received will be contributed to ALS (Lou Gehrig's
disease) awareness, treatment, and prevention.*

On the cover: (Historic image courtesy Nashua Historical Society, contemporary image taken by Robin
Ann Peters.)

CONTENTS

ACKNOWLEDGMENTS

Each year, the White House News Photographers' Association competes together for recognition in a contest called "The Eyes of History." As a photographer and a historian of Nashua, this book is the creative and documentary result of my "Eyes of Nashua History." Then & Now: *Nashua* was researched and formulated between April 2004 and the late months of 2005.

In preparation for this book and over the past 20 months, I have taken over 7,500 photographs and researched over 200 subjects, current and historic, of Nashua. This project has provided me a great deal of opportunity and a gamut of experiences alongside each turn of the page, and each click of the shutter. The creation of Then & Now: *Nashua* has brought me much enjoyment, excitement, religion, friendships, patriotism, respect, inspiration, and fulfillment. I should not hasten to mention the blood, sweat, and tears also forged into the process of its completion.

The dedicated preservationists I have been in close contact with, being Alan S. Manoian, Frank R. Mooney, the Nashua Historical Society, and the Nashua Library, have all developed my historical studies and provided information and encouragement beyond my imagination. Thank you is just not enough.

"Then" photographs are categorized with special markings from each collection of their origin. Photographs listed FMC are from the Frank Mooney Collection; photographs with M/P are from the Mooney/Pickering Collection; all images with NHS are from the Nashua Historical Society; all photographs marked with NPL were added from the protected collection of the Nashua Public Library. All other photographs were created by myself, Robin Ann Peters, unless otherwise noted.

My sincere appreciation to contributors from the Nashua Historical Society: members Beth McCarthy, William Ross, Nancy Twaddell, and Margaret Garneau. Equal thanks of merit belong to Jodi Lowery-Tilbury, Matt Cosgro, Barbara Berrios, Maria Donetti and family, Linda and Henry Willett, Edmond and Aurore Dionne, and Ed Brousseau. Thank you all so much for your availability, patience, and submissions.

For the endowments from Florence C. Shepard, Clarke S. Davis and committee, Judge Edward E. Parker and committee, and Charles J. Fox, I present my deepest gratitude. The Nashua historical references from each begin, maintain, and improve the road of my Nashua history achievements.

To my publisher, and all the incredible people who work there with whom it is an incredible joy to labor with; to my great friend Michael L. Bouchard, for his continual emotional support and access to technology; to all the friends and families in Merrimack who provide kindness, support, and friendship to my children and me; to my entire family, especially those working at Gate City Fence Company, who provide loving support every day; and to everyone who has touched the life of this book. Thank you.

Most importantly, Then & Now: *Nashua* would not be complete without the strength, encouragement, understanding and love from my son and daughter. Cory and Hannah, you are the greatest joys in my life. Love, Mom.

God bless you all.

INTRODUCTION

The land of Nashua, New Hampshire, has been inhabited by hunters and collectors for at least 5,000 to 7,000 years. These American Indians stalked wild animals and the native salmon fish of the waters while also collecting fur, bone, and timber for survival. Today's modern hunters are company executives stalking business deals and their 21st century counterparts are collectively trying to preserve them. It seems the hunter is now the hunted, and the collection has been placed on the people instead of the instruments.

Society is finally taking a step back, to look beyond the business deal and think about the foundation that it was built upon. No longer can we tear it all down and give society a trendy makeover, which will satisfy our lifelong desires. The interests of today are shifting towards our heritage values. This is our opportunity to build upon what we already have and in the process carry on the spirit of the people who built the foundations, which will then remain with the men and women who preserve them.

Have you ever gone to visit a place of your youth only to find it has been torn down, leveled, or destroyed? There are historical, financial, and emotional costs—none is as evident as the 9/11 tragedy. Nashua has lost its share of treasures, and a limited collection to some of our most extraordinary fates is featured in a special chapter entitled Tribute.

So then we must make it our mission! Let us bring attention to our history and save the precious jewels of our heritage. As history enthusiasts and preservationists, we are the sounding voice to our communities. Let us find the stone bits and brick pieces that make our city great! Saint Joseph's hospital recycled almost 100 percent of their original bricks when they tore down a great portion of the original building and expanded the facility in 1969–1970. Citizens have rallied together to save historic buildings such as the Mine Falls Gate House and the Saint Francis Xavier Church. To our dismay, a day must come where some will fall. Progress is a nice word. But change is its motivator. And change has its enemies. Robert F. Kennedy said that about progress, and I am a firm believer change is good, very good for that matter. But let us look intently at what we are changing before we start tearing things apart.

The research within these pages to what has been preserved and what has been lost looks upon the strength of the century-old foundations that still stand in our city today. Studying in the Hunt Room of the Nashua Library, in the home of a private collector, making personal interviews of new and old-time residents, and attending the Nashua Historical Society as a new member have also contributed facts to the parables contained in these pages. This historic research and preservation is a story that can be shared by generations, for generations.

To begin to understand Nashua properly, one must first become accustomed to the metamorphosis of its name. Throughout history books, pages are lined with references to Nashua, Nashville, Dunstable, Old Dunstable, Upper Dunstable, and Indian names such as Nashuaway, Indian Head, and Wattananock.

For our purposes, we will start with October 26, 1673, when a rectangular shaped tract of land approximately 128,000 acres was chartered as the Massachusetts Bay Colony township of Dunstable. A very historic map of this area exists in many other Nashua historical references, which is why we chose not to include it in this publication.

One by one, over the course of the next 67 years after its charter, new towns set-apart from Dunstable, and the original 200 square mile territory became known as Old Dunstable.

By 1740, only the land that contains the current Nashua, New Hampshire, and Tyngsboro, Massachusetts, remained with the Dunstable name. The Massachusetts and New Hampshire state line had not yet been created, and the royal commission of England appointed to define it could not agree to its proper placement; so the question went before the king in council, George II. When the line was finally drawn in 1741, his decision encapsulated the exact embodiment of land now known today as Nashua, New Hampshire.

For nearly 100 more years, Nashua kept the name of Dunstable. The towns of Dunstable, New Hampshire, and Dunstable, Massachusetts, were regularly confused, so the name Upper Dunstable was also used for distinction.

It was not until the high-spirited and momentous oration from the historic and prominent citizen Daniel Abbot of Indian Head Village in 1803 that inspired the town to change its name to Nashua. He and members of the settlement christened the first riverboat equipped for regular transportation of goods the *Nashua* and henceforth the area was then also known as Nashua Village.

Now prior to any formal English settlement to this area, the indigenous tribe of the Penacook's lived, traded, and traveled on the Nashuaway (Nashua) River. Later, industrialists from the 19th century brought mills to this same river to begin Nashua's social and economic developmental ascent. Nashua, officially named on December 31, 1836, is the proud designation derived from the river so vital to its founding inhabitants.

Nashville came about when a monumental disagreement between the northern and southern settlers of this area occurred. On June 23, 1842, a dissection act was passed for the northerners and so everything north of the Nashua River was made into "a separate and corporate town to be known by the name of Nashville." The towns would remain separated for 11 years, until 1853, when they would rejoin as one city, the City of Nashua.

Whichever name is read or heard, there is a spirit in our land that will always contain its changing and everlasting characteristics. It can be felt through the tumultuous times of our floods, fires, and tribulations all the way to our triumphs, trophies, and jubilations. It can be seen in the strength of our largest trees and in our architectural pinnacles; it can be heard in the halls of our churches, our schools, and our legislature. Then & Now: *Nashua* is now your journey into a great part of the dynamic spirit of Nashua, New Hampshire.

During World War II, the Nashua Manufacturing Company produced some of the finest materials produced that were used in the war for our soldiers. The Nashua Manufacturing Company was recognized for excellence with the Army-Navy "E" Award. (Courtesy NHS.)

Chapter 1

LANDMARKS

All endeavor calls for the ability to tramp the last mile,
shape the last plan, endure the last hours toil.
The fight to the finish spirit is the one characteristic we must
posses if we are to face the future as finishers.
—Henry David Thoreau (1817–1862),
American writer

The Soldiers and Sailors Monument was dedicated on Veterans Day, October 15, 1889. Col. Frank G. Noyes of Nashua, orator to the Memorial Day delegations for the forthcoming monument, had this to say about its symbolism: "We here deposit in this cornerstone, memorials of our day and age . . . to perpetuate the memory of those who offered their lives upon the altar of their country, and to be constant, though silent reminder of their patriotism, heroism and devotion." Day and night, city traffic noisily passes by the silent memorial to the 1,355 Nashua soldiers and sailors of the war of the rebellion of 1861–1865. A small road behind the remembrance grounds offers short refuge to those who wish to behold the Goddess of Liberty atop the 52 foot, 8 inch memorial, although a short walk to the historical society offers endless opportunity. (Historic image courtesy FMC.)

Citizens and governing officials are seen here entering the city hall just moments after its grand opening on November 20, 1939. It is said the pioneer leaders in the 17th century gathered together in a meetinghouse made from logs. A very famous meetinghouse was called "the Old South," and was built in 1812. Records from a town meeting in March 1842 record two rival groups of men in heated conversation with regard to a suitable location for a proper townhouse. Proponents living north of the river were unanimous in the opinion "if they had to cross the river at all they would just as soon go the whole distance to the Old South meetinghouse." So it was put to a vote, and the north side lost by a narrow margin. This one event caused such a sharp division in the townsmen that the northerners gathered together in separate government and formed the separate town of Nashville. (Historic image courtesy NHS.)

This is a very rare view of the Nashua Manufacturing Company taken before Mill No. 7 (1904) and the clock tower (1913) were added to the east side. The 21st century image of Clocktower Place shows the complete mill structure where, in 1944, when the company was in full operation, there were about 1,000 operatives working within, consuming 10,000 bales of cotton and producing approximately 13 million yards of cloth per annum. Prior to Mill No. 7, the three mills were producing 9.3 million yards per year. This was still 50 times faster than cloth created by hand. Mill No. 1 was completed in 1825, however it burned in 1856 and was rebuilt in 1857; Mill building No. 2 was built and in partial operation in 1827, reaching full operation in 1828; Mill building No. 3 was completed in 1836. Today the mill buildings are a series of apartments, completed in the late part of the 20th century. (Historic image courtesy NHS.)

On June 18, 1823, a charter for the Nashua Manufacturing Company gave permission to "Manufacture cotton, woolen and iron goods, and conduct other business and trade could be conveniently managed, on and near the Nashua River in Dunstable." Locating the factory at the head of Mine Falls was considered but quickly disregarded as it was too far from the Merrimack River and other transportation methods. The three-mile long Nashua canal began powering Mill No. 1 in 1825. Restorations of the Gate House at the falls began in 1997. Mary Coe, a Nashua school teacher, was thrust into the limelight of this restoration project after Alan Manoian was called to begin other Nashua projects. Coe has continued the restoration

project with federal, state, and local government entities along with students, volunteers, and veteran members of the Student Historic Preservation Team. (Historic image courtesy FMC.)

In September 1826, 87 respected townsmen with noble wishes to liberate Christianity signed a document forming the First Unitarian Congregational Society of Dunstable. Asher Benjamin, agent to the Nashua Manufacturing Company and America's firstborn architect, was responsible for its design. The pillar pedestals lining the front are complete fallen oaks from the Gage wood-lot in Bedford and driven to Nashua by a team of oxen. A first set of logs, fallen from Bow and floated down the Merrimack, were rejected because they were not large enough. Between 1928 and 1929, the entire structure was lifted and moved eastward several feet to accommodate the creation of the Parish House on its west. The new location is evident by the odd placement of the front door to the front steps, which were originally built to line up together. (Historic image courtesy NHS.)

The first record of church activity in Nashua is a charter granted by the Massachusetts legislature in 1673 to organize. It was not until December 16, 1685, when seven men would formally organize the church in this photograph, the First Church, then called the First Church of Christ in Dunstable. The church building seen here would not be completed until 1894; large donations were made by Lucy Kendall Spaulding, Isaac Spaulding's widow; Mary Park Nutt, benefactor of the 15-bell chime in its belfry originally created for the 1893 World's Fair; and Ella F. Anderson who donated an organ in memory of her husband. Helen Keller visited First Church in 1933. (Historic image courtesy FMC.)

The First Baptist church was built in 1849 at a cost of $18,000. History has it recorded where the first church building of this congregation was built, on this same corner lot in 1833, however, it was destroyed in a terrific fire named by the townspeople "The Great Fire of 1848." This photograph was taken after 1893, since the Whiting building can be viewed on the right side of the image. The church at 34 Main Street is currently in use by the Grace Fellowship Ministries. Over the past nine years, Grace Fellowship has expanded services and offices into the Franklin Mill building, at 55 Franklin Street, and because of space limitations in the original church, services are also given in the Elm Street Junior High School auditorium. (Historic image courtesy M/P.)

Prior to 1910, this church was the first home to the Irish-Catholics of Nashua. Completed in 1857 without a steeple, it was dedicated and named the Church of the Immaculate Conception Parish. In 1907, Bishop Guertin sent Rev. Leo Tyllo to serve the growing Lithuanian community who were meeting there with greater regularity. When Saint Patrick's church was completed in 1909, a sale was made to the Lithuanians and this became the Saint Casmir church. The photograph below was taken just days before a construction company began gutting its interior. When asked about reconstruction details, the foreman for the jobsite gave his admiration and respect for the men of that era who had only their bare hands and farm animals to help them construct a building, which by today's standards is "in perfect structural condition." (Historic image courtesy FMC.)

William Woodruff, bishop of the New Hampshire Diocese in 1870, organized a mission to Nashua under the name the Church of the Good Shepherd. The Episcopalian parish was still struggling from the decision, which closed the Saint Luke church in 1868, enforced under the decision from the previous Bishop Carlton Chase. A gift "In memory of a beloved and sainted daughter," from Mrs. Rand of Middletown, Connecticut, was given to the church in 1878, and so the church was built on the Main Street lot, which was obtained for an additional $65,000 by Rev. Jacob LeRoy and Bishop Woodruff. Today, Rev. Dr. Robert "Odie" Odierna, rector, was instrumental in the creation of the Nashua Pastoral Care Center, Nashua's premier outreach program, in 1987. It now has its own budget of over $1 million. (Historic image courtesy NHS.)

The first Jewish families to settle in Nashua date back to the late 1880s. In 1889, 25 men chartered Bace Abraham "for charitable, benevolent, and religious purposes." On July 12, 1899, the *Nashua Telegraph* announced the "First Synagogue in NH to be Erected Here." Immigration persisted during the early 1900s, the Ladies Aid Society was formed to help newcomers, and, by 1927, conversation of enlarging the current synagogue or moving to a larger structure had begun. The necessity for an updated and expanded synagogue and religious center was set into motion in 1951 after Rabbi Fischer introduced the "Couples Club." In 1955, Philip Porter donated a large lot on Raymond Street and helped organize the raising of funds to create what would become Temple Beth Abraham, completed in 1960. (Historic image courtesy Temple Beth Abraham.)

The parking area and waterfront to the Nashua River below the Water Street ramp was redesigned in 1998 into a riverfront park. The park, named Le Parc de Notre Renaissance Française, was dedicated in 2001 by the city in cooperation with leaders of the French-Canadian community. A monument of a woman, with book and child, stands before the river, commemorating the many Nashua mill workers, especially the Nashua "mill girls" who, throughout the antebellum decades, helped build this city. Books were not allowed in the mills, so education was placed into one's own expense. Many mill girls formed reading and writing groups that culminated into scholar schools and ultimately inspired Nashua's higher education and high schools.

The Goodrich building, present on the corner of Water and Main Streets, dates this photograph to somewhere before the 1920s when it burned and was soon after demolished. (Historic image courtesy NHS.)

The Laton Hotel building in Railroad Square is Nashua's oldest original surviving hotel structure. Prior to the Laton, a hotel named the Merrimac House, which was known previously as the Central House, occupied the land. The 1831 Central House was originally located in what is now known as Deschene's Oval and was built to provide accommodations for travelers to the depot station at Railroad Square. In 1845, the land in the Oval was sold to the city and the building was moved to its current site. As the town and station grew, the need for a larger hotel was facilitated in 1881 by the Laton family, who purchased the Central House and property in 1876 to create the legendary Laton Hotel. (Historic image courtesy NHS.)

The Indian Head National Bank is pictured here in the southeast corner of the Whiting building. Upon the buildings completion in 1893, the bank immediately occupied the street level southern corner, since they had outgrown their previous quarters in the Depot building across the street. This picture was taken after the appearance of Frank Julian Sprague's first Electric Car in 1888 and before the bank moved into the Telegraph block in 1909. Nashville, Indian Head Village, and Nashua Village are all names known to this historic area. At 11:20 p.m. on the eve of January 20, 2005, small speckles of light in the Holiday Tree and globes of illumination in the city streets quietly glittered through a fine cascade of snowflakes falling lightly to the earth.

The calm cool air of the evening was brisk and clear, and the sound of traffic signals clicking from red to green could be heard. (Historic image courtesy NHS.)

The Central Fire House was built in 1870 and dedicated on February 9, 1871. There are only four occasions where historians of this city can pinpoint patriotic decorations such as those seen here: in 1888 there was a huge semi-military pageant with several hundred uniformed companies and bands, the city was thronged with delegates from the United States and Canada; in October 1889, during the Soldiers and Sailors Monument dedication; in June 1903, the city celebrated its semi-centennial anniversary; and lastly, during the 75th anniversary celebration in 1928. The old photograph of the Central Fire House is not dated. Today the firehouse is used by artists and musicians for practice and performance. (Historic image courtesy NHS.)

On May 14, 1891, the cornerstone for the Odd Fellows Building was laid into the lot of the 1828 Colburn home; the occasion for its formal dedication was celebrated on April 26, 1892. The Odd Fellows Building is a classic Richardson Romanesque Revival; the second and third floors on the Main Street side are accented with Chicago windows, the window style popularized from the Illinois school of architects during the turn of the 19th century. The Odd Fellows Building was renovated and renamed the Landmark Building in 1982. The Hampshire Driving School, Nashua's oldest school for learning how to drive, may be its oldest tenant. For about 32 years, instructors have been riding in Nashua traffic teaching the budding motorists of our community. (Historic image courtesy NHS.)

This view of the Main Street Masonic temple was taken very soon after construction was completed in 1891. John Lund, Alfred Greeley, Joel Thayer, Thomas French, Joel Nason and William Cogswell,

organizers of the Nashua Masons, met in homes and a small meeting house on the corner of Olive and Temple Streets while planning the Nashua order. When the Olive Street church came down in 1881, a copper plate from the cornerstone inscribed with a message from the Grand Lodge of New Hampshire was collected and later ceremoniously placed into the cornerstone of this Masonic temple building in 1889. The Nashua Masons are still an active society of men with "principles and character," quoted from Mark Leavitt, past master mason of Ancient York Lodge No. 89 during an interview at the lodge office on the second floor in 2005. (Historic image courtesy Nashua Masons.)

This was the first dedicated Nashua courthouse after the reorganization of the state courts in 1866. Nashua, in the late part of the 19th century, had been made the Hillsborough County seat and was experiencing rapid municipal development. A new post office, police station, and a YMCA expanded the Main Street municipalities' center to the Court Street area. This section of Nashua is a very historic district, having also in its vicinity the Central Street Firehouse. Today the old courthouse keeps offices for the county attorney on the third floor, Nashua's registry of deeds on the second, and a satellite office for the Hillsborough County Sheriff on the first. The new superior courthouse building is located on Spring Street next to the newly renovated United States post office. (Historic image courtesy NPL.)

On August 3, 1877, eight Nashua church leaders, including Lester Freeman Thurber of the Pilgrim Congregational church, gathered together and created the YMCA (Young Men's Christian Association) organization in Nashua to provide fellowship, bible study, and educational instruction to area young men. Rooms for members at 69 Main Street and a gymnasium on Water Street were used before the Spring Street location (pictured) was built. Pres. William Howard Taft, 27th president of the U.S. (1909–1913), visited Nashua on March 12, 1912, to lay the cornerstone in this YMCA building. In 1964, YMCA joined with the YWCA to build a sports and recreational club on Prospect Street, which is still popular today. The YMCA building on Spring Street is now privately owned and no longer affiliated with YMCA. It is currently being used as a rooming house. (Historic image courtesy NPL.)

Health care in Nashua began with one Boston-printed medical publication, written by Dr. Thomas Thacher, who was also pastor in Nashua's Old South Church. Prior to 1700, this was the only medical book in New England. After much time and education, resident physicians along with town officials organized dedicated care centers in 1893, 1899, and in 1915 when Memorial Hospital was completed. In 1908, Saint Joseph's Hospital, pictured here before their 1915 addition, was dedicated by Bishop Guertin and Father Millette of the Saint Louis de Gonzague Church. Nine Sisters from the Order of Canada came to Nashua as administrators and staff to the new hospital and nursing school. Saint Joseph's Hospital underwent a major addition and

reconstruction in 1967–1970, where original bricks were torn down by hand and recycled. Saint Joseph's Hospital was expanded again in 2005–2006. (Historic image courtesy NPL.)

C. H. Avery, cofounder of Avery's Furniture, formed a partnership with C. R. Pease in 1887, specializing in stoves and home furnishings. Prior to his partnership with Pease and for 16 years earlier, Avery was a clerk for Charles W. Howard, a long-time furniture businessman in Milford and Nashua. Pease and Avery occupied three storefronts on Factory Street and had extensive rear rooms filled mainly with furniture. Pease was better adapted to stoves and by 1891, he had separated from Avery to pursue his own interests. This photograph is dated 1926 and was taken before the Pinets took ownership of the store around 1940. In 1992, they sold ownership to father-and-son, Robert and Steve Lavoie. When Bob Lavoie was asked what the future holds for Avery's, he simply stated with a genuine smile, "Maintain and expand the business!" (Historic image courtesy Avery Furniture.)

Herbert Rasmus McDonald located a tinsmith business at 73 Factory Street in 1889. In the year 1900, he relocated to 11 Factory Street specializing in stoves and plumbing. After hiring Hiram F. Rolfe in 1905, he moved to 7 Factory Street where he and Rolfe conducted business together until 1935. Kitchen furnishings were the specialty beginning around 1925. Hiram brought his two sons Leonard and Donald into the company during the 1940s and 1950s and his grandson Duane in the 1970s. Brother and sister Judy and Duane Rolfe, the current proprietors, provide a multiplicity of kitchenware. The collection and the McDonald legacy may very well soon belong to the tribute section of this

book as the Rolfe blood line contains no more heirs. Judy Rolfe believes the business will be liquidated after she and her brother can no longer care for the store. (Historic image courtesy FMC.)

31

Pennichuck Water Works was originally in 1852 the "Nashville Aqueduct." The water company has relied upon the Pennichuck Brook and five reservoir ponds, which feed it to serve the growing needs of this area, for 154 years now. Many people are involved and interested in the fresh water supply of Nashua; a watershed council, whose purpose is to save the land that filters the supply; governing officials in the city, who are trying to purchase the water company; and construction historians, who in the 1970s designated the institution with an award as a historical site for Civil Engineering. High controversy surrounds the fate of Pennichuck Water Works and its natural watershed. The current owners have made the alterations seen in the updated photograph.

The Works Progress Administration began construction on Holman Stadium in 1936 and completed with a formal dedication on September 23, 1937, the designer was Phillip S. Avery. Frank Holman, a key benefactor to the project, contributed $55,000 in honor of his parents. Charles Holman, Frank's father, is a success story of a man who came to Nashua sometime in the 1800s, started and maintained what became a successful confectioners business on Eldridge Street, and was also elected mayor of the city. This photograph was taken on June 10, 2005, with 3,493 in attendance at the annual Nashua Pride night for the Merrimack Youth Association. The highlight of the evening, receiving the highest amount of cheers, was the fireworks display after the game with popular orchestrations from movies such as *Harry Potter* and *Star Wars*. (Historic image courtesy FMC.)

This is the first public library building erected by Nashua. The John M. Hunt Memorial Building is the culmination of good intentions and bitter realities. After a fantastic gift of $50,000 was placed into the project by Hunt's wife Mary A. and daughter Mary E. in 1892, problems persisted for more than 10 years, similar to those that had caused the town to break apart in 1842. The building was finally completed in 1903 without ceremonial dedication, as none could bring adequate celebration to make up for the disconcerting events of its creation. Today the building is cared for by city appointed trustees and is available for special events. (Historic image courtesy NHS.)

This Queen Anne–Victorian on Concord Street, dressed in patriotic spirit, is forever a symbolic salute to patriots and the country. (Courtesy NHS.)

Our sweetest experiences of affection are meant to point us to that realm which is the real and endless home of the heart.
—Henry Ward Beecher (1813–1987),
American clergyman

This home is known as the 1700 House, the Blodgett House, the Killicut House, the Killicut-Way House, and is often referred to as the oldest house in Nashua. Originally the house was addressed on East Dunstable Road, however, it has been purposely overgrown on its north side and a new entry was especially created. There seems to be a lot of controversy with regard to the actual construction date for this home. Several people allude to its erection date based upon word of mouth stories and such. No date or year has ever been confirmed. From an architectural perspective, this house is clearly not from the year 1700. Its design, a cape-style Georgian, was not built prior to 1725. Considering it is close to 300 years old, give or take a few decades, it is in remarkably good shape and is currently still used as a residence by two very caring owners. (Historic image courtesy FMC.)

This house is historically known as "the Haunt." The Haunt is a traditional Georgian Colonial. It was originally built in 1740 on the shores of the Nashua River. While boating on the river, William Spaulding took a liking to the saltbox and had it moved in 1896 to the land on his Concord Street address. In 1906, both buildings on 27 Concord Street were sold at auction. A separate road was added later to gain access to the Haunt, and it was then again made into a primary residence. The current owners have restored many parts of their home, and still have more of the original pieces waiting in storage. (Historic image courtesy Henry and Linda Willett.)

William Spaulding was known for his enthusiastic practice of collecting antiques and the little house he picked up from the Nashua River was a nice addition, in which to showcase them. Spaulding had to restore the exterior and interior as it was in a sad state of disrepair when he purchased it. This image of a first floor room was taken during the Spaulding's ownership; it gives a glimpse of the preservation and decor present at the beginning of the 19th century. The current owners kindly allowed a recreation of this rare interior view in this treasured historic home, which is almost three centuries old. Its original builder was Deacon William Cummings. (Historic image courtesy FMC.)

This house was built in 1800 by John Lund and resident to the honorable Daniel Abbot, Nashua lawyer and businessman, in 1803. Dunstable was then a humble population of about 900, and his home lay in almost unbroken forest. The only highways existing at that time were the Amherst and Concord roads, Main Street, and a road down the northern bank of the Nashua River to the boathouses and ferries. Daniel Webster was a frequent visitor to Abbot here. William Spaulding bought the house in 1906 and set out to restore it. He lived there for many years. The Nashua Historical Society bought the Abbott–Spalding house in 1978. The house was listed on the National Register of Historical Places in

1980 through dedicated perseverance of members of the society. (Historic image courtesy NHS.)

This is 39 Orange Street, the first brick residence north of the Nashua River. It was constructed in the early 1830s for a young Solomon Spaulding; he was only 23. Spaulding was a merchant and eventually partnered with Henry Stearns in 1857.

Later, he became president of the New Hampshire Banking Company, a small Nashua bank, which operated from 1879 to 1895. According to Frank Ingalls, famed Nashua photographer, in about the year 1876 when this photograph was taken, Spaulding had become a Judge and still occupied this house. Although Ingalls did not create this image, he did print it from an original negative. He later created at least one other photograph of this house dated by his hand on January 5, 1941, when Ned Whittemore was the homeowner. (Historic image courtesy NPL.)

Number 37 Orange Street was built by John Reed, 166 years ago for the Stearns family, in 1840. The Stearns family resided in this house for almost 150 years. Anna Stearns was born within and lived her whole life as resident of the home; she died recently at the age of 90. This "then" picture is a copy of an original stereoscopic view taken by Samuel C. Hamilton, a photographer listed in the city directories from 1864 to 1865 at 69 Factory Street. Henry Stearns and Solomon Spaulding were neighbors and business partners dealing dry goods from a store in Railroad Square with an additional storage warehouse located at 117 East Hollis Street in the early 1900s. Jesse Stearns is listed

as owner of the house in a 1925 city directory. A Stearns block building is still located in Railroad Square. (Historic image courtesy FMC.)

The land for this home, on 27 Concord Street, was originally sold from the Nashua Manufacturing Company to Alfred Greeley on April 4, 1828, for the sum of $500.

Alfred Greeley was not related to Joseph Thornton Greeley, the man who in 1881 willed his entire farm on Concord Street to the City of Nashua. J. T. Greeley is a descendant of Mathew Thornton, the Londonderry and later Merrimack resident who signed the Declaration of Independence. There were six owners to this house prior to the purchase made by William E. Spaulding on May 29, 1888. Ten other owners occupied this house after Spaulding and prior to the current owners who bought 2 Davis Court (also known as 27 Concord Street) on November 3, 1981. The current decor is in a contemporary opus; ample window light, sculptural furnishings, art, neutral elements and bold color flow through the first floor rooms. (Historic image courtesy NHS.)

The home of Isaac Spaulding was built in 1852 and was the first residence in Nashua with running water. Isaac Spaulding was a well-known Nashua merchant who later became equally successful in railroading, banking, and politics. Upon his death in 1876, Spaulding was considered the wealthiest man in all of New Hampshire. His home today is obstructed by a commercial business block, which does provide a wide corridor between Chuck's Barber Shop and Gate City Coin and Jewelry to the front door. Charles Aveni started his barber shop in June of 1959, on Main Street in the building that has been newly renovated in 2005 into the Peddler's Daughter Restaurant and Pub. On September 10, 1984, 25-year employee Rino R. Long bought Chuck's barbering business and moved it to this location in the

middle of the downtown, in front of Spaulding's house. (Historic image courtesy NHS.)

Significantly displayed between Manchester and Concord Streets is the Stark House. This architectural vista displaying classic Italianate influence has survived from 1853 when it was built for George Stark, great-grandson of Bennington war hero Gen. John Stark. George Stark was a surveyor and engineer's assistant during his school vacations,

he later pursued an active role in railroad development and eventually became superintendent of the Nashua and Lowell Railroad and all of its branches. The Stark House was the third property listed with the National Register of Historic Places. There are currently five Nashua properties and two Nashua districts on the national registry; the Abbot-Spaulding House, the John M. Hunt Memorial Library, the Killicut-Way House, the Gen. George Stark House, the Nashua Manufacturing Company Historic District, and the Nashville Historic District. (Historic image courtesy FMC.)

The Farwell Funeral Home on Lock Street between Granite and Orange Streets was originally built for Col. Thomas P. Pierce, comrade of famed Nashua Patriot Gen. John G. Foster. Foster moved to Nashua with his parents at the age of 10, was schooled here, and later accepted to West Point with a prestigious recommendation from Nashua Congressman Charles G. Atherton. He was the captain of many military companies and traveled throughout the United States and other countries in service to his own. This late-1800s mansion was built upon Foster's lot after his house was moved to the corner of Lock and Dow Streets in 1870. Frank D. Laton also lived in this residence some time later. Frank Ingalls took this "then" photograph in 1941. (Historic image courtesy NHS.)

This Queen Anne–Victorian home is located at 86 Concord Street. Constructed around 1890, this home was purchased by the Nashua Children's Home, an organization that has been providing individualized care and stability to Nashua boys and girls of difficult or adverse situations since 1899. This house is used for girls, and a location on Amherst Street is used for boys. Organized in 1903 as the Protestant Orphanage Association, it was known as the Nashua Children's Association from 1970 until 1998. Public and private donations, including a donation of at least $25,000 from the City of Nashua's Community Development Block Grant, helps to fund this rescue organization for disadvantaged Nashua children. (Historic image courtesy NHS.)

This photograph, taken sometime between 1868 and 1877, of the lumber sheds, box shop, and office of Sargent and Cross mills was created by the 1842 cyanotype photographic method. This is the intersection of Nashua Street (the road crossing the railroad tracks) and Canal Street (the wide road in the upper left) near their lot on the Nashua River. (Courtesy NPL.)

Chapter 3

STREETS

Men make their own history, but they do not make it just as they please; they do not make it under circumstances chosen by themselves, but under circumstances directly found, given, and transmitted from the past.
—Karl Marx (1818–1883) German economist, philosopher, and author; from letter to Joseph Wedemeyer, March 5, 1852

This mid-1900s birds-eye view of Main Street has been a popular spot for Nashua photographers for

many years. On the eve of the ninth annual Downtown Nashua Winter Holiday Stroll, R. A. Peters embarked up the little-used spiral staircase to reach the John M. Hunt Memorial Building watchtower roof with A. S. Manoian, the man who created the stroll event while employed with the city. As the throng of spirited Nashuans moved upon the holiday tree from city hall, Manoian was riveted by the tide of candles approaching, while Peters exposed frame after frame of film with her Bronica SQA camera. A few images were also saved on a borrowed AGFA digital camera, as this was the year of her birth unto digital photography. (Historic image courtesy NHS.)

Business blocks dominate this street scene north of Temple Street around the beginning of the 19th century. The Landmark Building is the large dominant structure on the immediate left in the photograph, across Temple Street is the Telegraph building and block, a distinct Second Empire structure. On the right are the First National Bank building, the Goddard, the Ridgeway, and the Beasom building. Across Factory Street is the Hunt building, the Noyes, and then the Union building in that order. Just south of the Pearl Streets and beyond the slightly visible porches on the front of the Tremont House, the road narrows east to about half its apparent width between the Odd Fellows building and the Beasom block, in the foreground of this old photograph. Pictured in the

"now" photograph is the west side of Main Street in the area just south of West Pearl Street to West Hollis Street, where in the old photograph is seen completely undeveloped. (Historic image courtesy FMC.)

Montgomery Ward was a home goods national chain store on Main Street for many years in the 1900s, while the First National Store next door was the largest supermarket in the city. There was a large bakery in the rear of the building, which supplied another branch location on Lake Street. Directly north (on the right) of these two buildings in these photographs, is the historic Shea building, constructed in 1926, it had the tenants of Damon Real Estate (now located at 204 A Main Street), the Nashua Chamber of Commerce (now located at 151 Main Street) and in 1935 Aubuchon Hardware (who is still a tenant today). The Archambeault family has been running the hardware store for almost the entire 71 years. This photograph was taken around 1939, the first car in view in front of the supermarket is a Chevrolet Sedan sporting the new trunk which was the automobile's latest feature.

This late-19th-century photograph can be pinpointed to sometime between 1872, when the Merchants Exchange building was completed, and 1876, after Gilman Scripture added porches to the front of the Tremont Hotel. The Noyes building at the far right occupies the space where the Washington Hotel stood from 1830 to 1853. The Exchange building looks very similar to its 1888 predecessor, largely due to a historic restoration completed on January 6, 1989, which included the new Martha's Exchange restaurant. Martha's is a popular gathering place, especially during the holidays. Their Thanksgiving Eve Reunion Party and New Years Eve

Celebration have become a Fokus family and well-liked tradition. (Historic image courtesy NPL.)

In 1888, the year of this photograph, the front of the Tremont Hotel was alongside the Merchants Exchange building, and a livery situated at the rear of the Tremont had an enterprising stable of about 40 horses where year round single and double teams could be rented. The horsecar seen riding towards the viewer is possibly headed to the Union Station to meet trains heading north and south. In Nashua, stagecoaches first began in 1795, horsecars in 1886, and the electric car began operations on July 27, 1895, with the first trip being from Nashua to Lowell, Massachuettes. The 1922 Second National Bank building in the "now" photograph was known as the Bank of New Hampshire for many years. Before the Tremont, a hotel named the Pearl Street House was resident to the bank's site. (Historic image courtesy FMC.)

Dr. Evan B. Hammond, with his home a residence just north of the Universalist church, was a devoted citizen with a strong sense to the community. His son also became a doctor in town and "always made Nashua his home, keeping his father's office as his own." William H. Beasom, Nashua mayor in 1891–1892, lived next door alongside the very wealthy Nashua businessman Isaac Spaulding, whose home was nearest to the Methodist church. Spaulding's business documents, currently on record with Frank Mooney, record the exact day of the separation and reunion of Nashua and Nashville. Pompanoosuc Mills now occupies the first floor of the Professional Building on the Hammond lot, the Chase building was built upon the Beasom residence in 1916. The great architrave for the Tremont Theatre is still visible on the second floor. (Historic image courtesy NHS.)

From the rooftop of the Masonic temple, a clear view of the Merchants Exchange building and south side of the Professional Building are predominant in the foreground. The Noyes block, center left side in the "then" photograph, provided mid-20th century Nashuan's a pleasant location for ice-cream sundaes in Priscilla's Tea Room after shopping at Brockerman's food market and before catching the bus home. Martha's Sweet Shoppe is still on Main Street, only now one must enter Martha's Exchange restaurant to reach the sweets! The Bank of America and the Nashua Chamber of Commerce occupy the brick building across from the Methodist church. Nashua's Main Street underwent a major face-lift in 1981, where brick was laid into sidewalks and trees were planted for shade and beauty. (Historic image courtesy City of Nashua.)

The Greeley block building was the northern Main Street focal point of Union Square for almost 70 years. In 1833, the Greeley brothers constructed this building along with two others on the land of the John M. Hunt Memorial Library building. The Greeley's, among other things, were part of the Nashua Coalition with Entrepreneurial Bostonians who with financiers were preparing to build the Nashua Mills in 1825. This 1800s Landmark Building remarkably still exists, it was moved in 1903 about 200 feet east to make way for the library. The Greeley building has contained many businesses along the way and also served as Nashville's Town Hall for some time. The "then" photograph was taken before the Old Chocolate

church (on the right) burned in 1870. The "now" photograph shows how the library building has reshaped Main Street and Railroad (Union) Square. (Historic image courtesy NPL.)

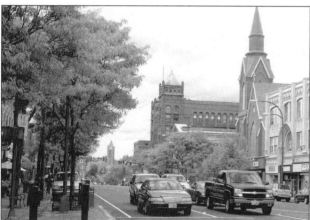

Isaac Spaulding's house (1852), the Methodist church (1868), the Telegraph block (1870), the Odd Fellows Building (now known as the Landmark Building 1892), some homes, and the Congregational church (home to the First Church in 1872) lined the east side of Main Street during the late 1800s in this old photograph. Today the Indian Head Bank building is still standing on the site where it was built in 1923 soon after the fire in the Telegraph block. The Nelson building, a little further in the distance, would not be erected until 1904. The Chase building was erected in 1916. From the dates of all the prominent structures in this old picture, the image can be dated between 1894 and 1922. (Historic image courtesy NHS.)

This is a Nashua Street Railway electric open car running south on Main Street in front of the Telegraph block and the Methodist church. Judging by the ivy on the church, the location of the photograph and the time span electric cars were used, this photograph was taken in the summer sometime between 1895 and 1922. There was trouble with open cars, as they could only be used during the warmer months. The Nashua Street Railway also had a closed car fleet for use in winter. Half the fleet was always in storage making the electric car business a risky enterprise, though its usefulness provided stability for the company until the advent and inherent domination by the automobile. (Historic image courtesy Matt Cosgro.)

Factory and Temple Streets were part of the original town layout created by Asher Benjamin, architect and first agent to the Nashua Manufacturing Company from 1825 to 1827. It was Benjamin's initial responsibility to provide a designed industrial complex on the land owned by the manufacturing company. He left nothing to chance, his design included the mill buildings and administrative offices, roads, trees, worker's housing, and religious facilities. He also aided to the design of the Nashua Canal. Prior to 1882, the Olive Street church building, which is said was also designed by Benjamin, stood on the lot at the top of Temple Street. The church in this photograph, the Pilgrim Congregational church, was built after the destruction of the Olive Street church. A fateful hurricane in 1954, caused enough damage to the Pilgrim church for the congregation to sell the lot in 1955 to the Indian Head Bank and move to a new church on Watson Street. (Historic image courtesy NHS.)

"We invite you to visit our store during 'BESSE WEEK' commencing September 24th, 1927 and compare the quality of our merchandise with the price tags. We assure you a pleasant and profitable surprise" was the 50th anniversary advertisement for Besse and Bryant's clothing store located on the corner of Factory and Main Streets. Since March 23, 1904, and prior to occupying the new construction of this building around 1923, the company was located in the Goddard building at 121 Main Street. Three days prior to the Besse and Bryant celebration, an earthquake was felt in Nashua. The Harvard astrological observatory reported the quake "to have been the most severe experienced in this section of the country since the memorable seismic disturbance of 1884." (Historic image courtesy NPL.)

This photograph, taken in the mid- to late 1800s, shows little sign of travel on Main Street. The "Great Road," as it was called so long ago, has manifested itself into a great throughway. Traffic congestion has been a problem now for decades. Plans are under investigation for the creation of a bypass, which would circumvent traffic away from historic downtown. Some opponents to the plan give reason not to proceed based upon the idea of continued preservation of historic mill properties west of Main Street. To preserve Main Street, as a traveled destination for tourists and locals and as an essential historic center, a road of circumvention is desperately needed to relieve damaging traffic and environmental

pressures for the businesses, buildings, and pedestrians of downtown. (Historic image courtesy FMC.)

William D. Beasom built the Beasom building on the corner of Main and Factory Streets around 1865. It was the home to many well-liked stores throughout its lifetime, including the Boston Clothing store in its early years, and later the Paris, and then Philip Morris. The Beasom block was hit several times by fire, the greatest being the fire in 1961 which finally removed the building completely. A new building was set on the Beasom block shortly thereafter called the Patriot Building. Tenants of the early 21st century include Stage Door Salon, which has occupied the south corner since it's erection; the San Francisco Kitchen, owned and operated by third generation restaurateur Stephanie Liang; Wingate's Pharmacy, a drugstore in operation since 1900; and Nashua Sports Collectibles, a sports fan store and agent for popular visiting sports figures. (Historic image courtesy FMC.)

This is Factory Street, one of the original streets created by the Nashua Manufacturing Company. Cale and Crane can be seen on the south side, and a bit further west on the north side you can see the business of E. G. Reed and E. A. Slater. There are many listings for E. G. Reed and A. G. Reed in the city directories. The two men were probably brothers, and from the listings it seems they were doing business together, with their father, and with several partners on different occasions from 1830 until 1870. E. G. Reed was most famous for his silver spoons. Factory Street today may very well be Nashua's most historic road for home furnishings. Both McDonald's Kitchenware and

Avery's Furniture have been located on this street since 1889. Avery's Furniture has been on the same lot the entire 117 years. (Historic image courtesy M/P.)

This view of the west side of Main Street was taken some time before 1872. It provides detail to the reasoning for the creation of the Montcalm, a crescent shape building which remained on Main Street until almost 1960. Three narrow business locations, the First National Bank, the Goddard building, and the Ridgeway, are together in a short row and are still visible today as Vow Wow's, the Garden, and Cardin's jewelry store. Next to the Ridgeway building is the Beasom block, and across High Street is the Hunt building, then the Noyes building, and finally far in the distance one can see a small amount of the Union building and the Tremont House, without its porches. Vow Wow's is located in the 1867 First National Bank building. The First National Bank merged in 1907 with the Second National Bank of 1873. Cardin Jewelers has been a family owned business in Nashua since the 1920s. (Historic image courtesy FMC.)

The Montcalm building, also known as the Crescent building, is now listed as the Howard building. It was built in the 1880s by Joseph W. Howard and his father, Ezra. The widening of Main Street began sometime in 1935, but all businesses up the east side of the street would not be completely removed until 1959. The church between Park and Pearson Streets, which burned down on February 20, 1967, has long since been removed. The Nelson building, constructed in 1904, still remains and is a very distinguished asset on Main Street. It contains very ornate features along the roofline and has distinguishable horizontal accents above and below the windows. Nelson

provided Nashua with the first Five-and-Dime, he was a very successful merchant during the early 1900s. (Historic image courtesy NHS.)

The first bridge across the Nashua River on Main Street was built in 1748. Trolley tracks are not visible on the street or bridge, which indicates this photograph is prior to 1885. A new bridge was created in 1825 due to the new Jackson Falls dam at Indian Head. The bridge had always required extensive maintenance due to traffic and washouts until it finally burned in December 1924. A temporary bridge was installed immediately for about a year until construction was finally completed in 1926. The bridge was remodeled in 1982. A 21st century sidewalk cleaning machine is moving about on the east side of the bridge. (Historic image courtesy M/P.)

The only structure remaining from this vintage photograph is the Methodist church, its steeple barely visible in the distance. The first townhouse followed by the Nutt building, the Phillips building, the First Congregational church, the Sargent building, and its neighbor, with the empty carriage out front, are all long departed. The Old Chocolate church of 1835 burned on April 15, 1870, and was reconstructed the same year to the more ornamented church building dominating this photograph. Charles C. Nutt left a large contribution for a hospital, which was contributed to Memorial Hospital towards a dedicated surgical center. The Phillips building was the first to hold a completely self-contained city post office, as prior all postal transactions were located in homes, stores, or inns. This photograph was taken prior to 1893. (Historic image courtesy NPL.)

The building lot on the northeast corner of Franklin Street originally had a home, which belonged to Robert Fletcher Esq. A temporary platform erected in front of Fletcher's dwelling provided Daniel Abbot, orator of a public address on July 4, 1803, a higher vantage position to deliver the days events to a great gathering of townspeople. Fletcher had recently completed Nashua's first canal boat, specifically designed for the regular transportation of goods. After a "rousing speech" from Abbot, the people of Nashua traveled to a place near the aperture of the Nashua River to the Merrimack River, to watch as Fletcher's "wonder boat" would enter the water for the first time. The boat was christened the *Nashua*, and the area known as the Indian Head Village henceforth was also called the Nashua Village. Ultimately, the city would get its everlasting name from this ephemeral event. (Historic image courtesy FMC.)

This is an open horse car running east on Canal Street in front of Railroad Square. A small portion of the Greeley building, the Laton building, and the west corner of the Laton Hotel can be seen beyond the horse and car. This photograph was taken between 1886 and 1895, while horsecars were in operation, electric cars would take over the lines in 1895. The Nashua Transit System began operations in 1979. Twenty-year employee and assistant director Lori Lorman has been with the Nashua Transit System almost its entire existence. She says, "I love the growth of our system. Ridership has increased, our employees are excellent and the passengers are great!" For

$1, you can gain access to one of five buses on six routes daily or one of the two buses which run each evening. (Historic image courtesy NPL.)

Three petitions to extend the Boston and Lowell Railroad Company to Nashua dated June 1, 1835, and signed by Dunstable citizens such as Daniel Abbott, Jesse Bowers, two of the Greeley brothers, and several other proponents, were addressed to the Senate and House of Representatives with requests "that if the facilities for conveyance were increased, the expenses would be lessened and the advantages of a market secured more equally to all . . ." The transportation wishes of Dunstable would be fulfilled on December 23, 1838, when the first railroad train traveled "all the way to Main Street" to the exact location of these photographs. The Nashua and Lowell city depot building on the left side of this *c.* 1920 photograph would not be built until 1849. (Historic image courtesy NPL.)

Archibald Harris Dunlap (September 2, 1817–April 5, 1894) was a fine and noble resident of Nashua. At the age of 19, he was employed at the Jackson Mills where he was promoted quickly to the position of overseer. His health failing, he had to leave the mills in 1847, but soon began a garden seed business in 1849 located in the building on the corner of Main and Fletcher Streets in this photograph. The garden seed business was quite successful due to his courageous and caring nature. With such a highly regarded reputation, he earned the trust of his fellow Nashua men and gained many honored selected positions such as railroad commissioner, presidential elector, alderman, and deacon in town. He

was also responsible for the calming resolution to the fitting location to the Soldiers and Sailors Monument, which had the town in quite a stir. (Historic image courtesy NPL.)

Looking south down Library Hill, this street car is making its way through the snow past the future site of the John M. Hunt Memorial Library. A lot of groundwork for the opportunity to borrow books from a public collection is contributed to a number of young women working together in 1867 calling themselves the Young Ladies Soldiers' Aid Society. Prior to this, a private library of 1,300 volumes was known as the Union Athenaeum. After many book drives, and with the advent and availability of bookstores (there were then four), the community began to desire the formation of a formal city public library. Leading men of the Athenaeum donated their collection to the city on the condition they should "forever maintain a free library." (Historic image courtesy NPL.)

The Old Congressional church, which was also home to the Park Theatre and Nashua Hardware, is shown here burning on February 20, 1967. It was completely devastated by the fire. (Courtesy FMC.)

Chapter 4

TRIBUTE

History is a story of growth, decay and change. If no provision, no allowance is made for change by peaceful means, it will come anyway—and with violence.
—Herbert Clark Hoover (1874–1964), American statesman (31st United States president: 1929–1933)

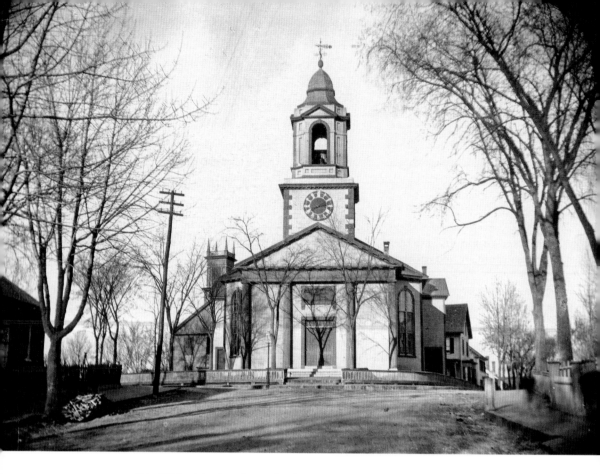

In 1825, this church was built as a meetinghouse by the Nashua Manufacturing Company for mill operatives. All were welcome; however the majority of attendants for religious services were Unitarians. On June 24, 1826, members of the congregational creed met separately

and agreed to worship together in a new building or possibly purchase "the Old South" meetinghouse at "the Harbor," and move it to new land of their own liking. The townspeople discussed many options, but when the Nashua Manufacturing Company made an offer to sell the 1825 meetinghouse to the Congregationalists for $5,000 they made the purchase. The house was dedicated on Wednesday, June 18, 1827, with Rev. Handell G. Nott ordained as minister. The right and left wings, clock, and bell were all added in 1837. In 1881, the church was sold at auction to Charles McGregor for $200. The Indian Head Plaza is the current occupant of this site. (Historic image courtesy NHS.)

This is Union Station, the most famous depot in Nashua during the railroading era. Six rail lines intersected here making this famed building the travel nucleus of the northeast. It was also known as the Nashua Junction and the Concord Depot. There are many conflicting dates with regard to the actual year of its construction. Smaller and temporary depots were also in use in this area while the lines were being developed; these other depots, along with the several names given to them, have created confusion and enhanced the possibility of historical error in researched transcriptions, which is why the actual date of it erection is not listed here. Some time into the mid-20th century, the station was no longer needed. The lot was made available and Howdy Beef Burger was the first to use the land. Drusilla Forrence Peters, a graduate from Saint Louis High School remembers "hanging

out" at the drive-in with her friends and boyfriend Harry C. Peters Jr. in the 1960s, ordering 5¢ hamburgers and 2¢ french fries. Several other restaurants have occupied the 1960s building. The property has gradually gone downhill, its current occupant is the Nashua Diner. The station was demolished in 1965. (Historic image courtesy FMC.)

UNION STATION   NASHUA, N. H

Amedee Deschene is recognized by the city for his valor in war. While stationed in Xivray, France, German troops rushed the line of his platoon through a thick fog—his battalion was greatly outnumbered. Upon what seemed to be an obvious loss, Private Deschene leapt up to the top of the trench and fired his Chauchot weapon into the German army. Deschene's automatic gun was one of few provided to the troops as it took a trained and capable hand to handle. He bravely stood into enemy fire and sent a waterfall of ammunition rounds into leader after German leader until all had fallen or retreated. His bravery and action surely saved his battalion from certain death and capture. The men standing at the World War I landmark are two of the six nephews to Amedee Deschene. Brothers Edmond Dionne, on the right, and Maurice Dionne, on the left, are sons to Amedee's sister Lydia. (Historic image courtesy FMC.)

In 1890, this medieval cobblestone structure was built as the headquarters to Nashua's first military. The Armory today is a storage and training facility and also home for the New Hampshire Army National Guard Recruiting and Retention Command office. The soldiers of Nashua Bravo Battery are trained to execute mass fires and destroy the enemy. Last year however, Battery B was called to Iraq to fulfill a different mission, additional training was secured at Fort Dix prior to their United States departure to Camp Bucca in Iraq. Duties included search and seizure, capture and detain combatants, security, and patrol missions. All members of the Nashua Battalion returned safely home and were greeted at the Manchester

airport with great commemoration. The original armory building on the corner of Canal and Grove Streets was destroyed by fire in 1957. The site is now occupied by the White Wing School (Historic image courtesy M/P.)

The cornerstone of the Saint Louis de Gonzague church was blessed by the bishop of the Portland, Maine, dioceses in May of 1872. Prior to the Reverend Jean Baptist Henry Victor Millet commencing the formation of a dedicated parish for the French community, the Catholics of Nashua were all registered at the Immaculate Conception Parish on Temple Street. As the French population grew between 1857 and 1870, religious and social interaction with the Irish-Americans proved worthy the need for an independent French-Catholic church. The original church building was lost by fire on the morning of July 20, 1976. The parish was able to save and incorporate the ornamental stained glass windows and some of the original doors from the burned building into the new church's construction. The small steeple from the 1872 original stands before its successor. At 3:00 p.m. on Sunday, February 4, 1979, the bishop of Manchester, principal celebrant under Pope John Paul II, sent word to his loyal attendants of the ceremony in the newly completed church building "we understand the meaning of this house of worship where Christians gather to be strengthened in their faith and rejoice in god's care for them." (Historic image courtesy FMC.)

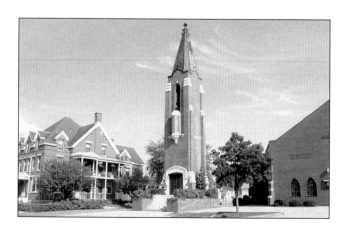

In 1845, Bishop Carlton Chase, the first bishop of New Hampshire, was petitioned by a few churchmen to send a clergyman to Nashua. Prior to building Saint Luke's church in the fork from Temple and East Pearl Streets to Main Street, the Episcopalian's in Nashua used private homes and the town hall to gather together. The bishop gave his blessing in 1857 for the construction of a house of worship. The church however, was of poor construction, and was also set somewhat beyond the normal routes, which made it quite inaccessible. These disadvantaged conditions led to a decreased attendance, and after 11 years of declining devotion, Bishop Chase ordered the closing of the church, and then also refused

to send any further clergyman. The congregation was forced to reestablish and form a new church, which would eventually lead to the creation of the Church of the Good Shepherd. (Historic image courtesy M/P.)

Samuel J. Bellavance Jr. and Joseph A. Bellavance IV are the newest owners of Bellavance Beverage Company, established by a Nashua family dating back to the late 1800s. On Friday, June 6, 1912, 50 cases of tonic on the cart in this photograph were set for delivery to a Good Cheer Society outing at Greeley Park. For years, the family also carried and distributed sodas such as popular "flavor-aged" Clicquot Club Cola, one possible reason the Bellavance company survived the prohibition law of January 16, 1920. As some of the Bellavance elders remember, "thugs" from Chicago arrived as messengers from Al Capone when the family stopped distributing his beer. The Bellavance's revived this old-time method of delivery this year; the world famous Budweiser Clydesdales delivered a carriage of fresh beer during the first annual "Get Fresh Downtown Nashua" event on May 26, 2005. Penuche's Ale House, a bar occupying the same property as the original Bellavance building, can be seen in the background. (Historic image courtesy Bellavance family.)

Solomon Spaulding was a merchant in Nashua in 1853, and in 1857, partnered with Henry Stearns. This store, in which they were partners, offered mostly dry goods and was in a convenient location at 15–16 Railroad Square, situated at the corner of Canal and Orange Streets. This photograph gives good representation of the items available in his store. The XXXX Pillsbury flour was not released until 1872, so this photograph must have been taken sometime after that. With grains, farmer supplies, and tobacco, this business remained in the Nashua marketplace until about 1903. The road to the right is Orange Street, where he retained a residence for many years. (Historic image courtesy M/P.)

A sawmill and gristmill were the first to employ the use of a dam on the Nashua River in 1815, near this part of the river. The sawmill of Sargent and Cross in this photograph, from 1868, was located here and is listed as moving to Quincy Street in 1877. In 1847 and 1878, deteriorated wood dams had to be repaired or replaced. The Jackson Company built the current dam of concrete coined the Jackson Falls Dam in 1907, and a power plant around 1920 to facilitate their cotton mill. Many restaurants have taken space in the upstairs of the late 1900s converted Jackson powerhouse, and in 1983, a hydroelectric plant was installed in its lower level. The most current tenant of this historic building is Margarita's, an American-Mexican culinary eatery with a large and popular bar space. (Historic image courtesy NPL.)

The Nashua Card and Glazed Paper Company began in 1869 when a small company, which manufactured glazed paper, partnered with three brothers in Nashua; Virgil C., Horace W., and O. B. Gilman. The "then" picture, made by Frank Ingalls, shows the shop building on Pearson Avenue that they used to make their products. In 1883, Bostonian H. H. Bixby bought out the firm as he saw a greater potential for the Card Shop, a name given to the business building by Nashua locals. His vision and entrepreneur skills landed the business a new facility on Franklin Street. These are the humble beginnings to Nashua Corporation, one of the largest and oldest companies from Nashua. The Carter family continued what Bixby

had started, and in the 20th century they moved to a larger facility in Merrimack where Nashua Corporation now experiences global recognition. (Historic image courtesy NPL.)

Newspaper publications began serving Nashua in 1826. The *Nashua Gazette*, as it would be renamed in 1831, was published on handmade paper until February 1828. The paper concluded its coverage on November 9, 1895. Other papers of Nashua included the *Nashua Oasis*, started by O. D. Murray; a French paper in the early 1900s under the name *L'Impartial*; the *NH Republican*, the *Nashua Herald*, and the *Granite State Register* also served Nashua with news for some time. Alfred Beard started the *New Hampshire Telegraph* in 1832, his paper took a strict Republican/Whig political stance against his democratic competitor Israel Hunt Jr. of the *Gazette*. His paper would transcend all into the 21st century as *The Telegraph*. *The Broadcaster* and *The Hippo* also have Nashua divisions that feature local news and advertisements in this century.

The Telegraph Block (1870) is a Second Empire style construction on the southwest corner of Temple Street. It was built to accommodate the launch of the daily edition of the *Nashua Telegraph* newspaper. A historical hall was set up by the Nashua Historical Society sometime before the devastating fire on March 14, 1922, which almost completely destroyed the building. The Indian Head Bank, previously known as the Nashua Bank, started in 1835 with Daniel Abbott as its first president. Upon its name change and incorporation on July 2, 1851, Joseph Greeley was elected president and the offices were located in the Central House in Railroad Square. After the Telegraph building burned, construction commencements began, but it would be another year before the completion of the prestigious

Indian Head building, which has become a historical landmark on Main Street. The law offices of Hamblett and Kerrigan are the current occupants. (Historic image courtesy NHS.)

Andrew E. Thayer, Federalist/Whig and Unitarian Congregational Church minister, ran the *Nashua Gazette* publication from 1829 until 1832, in the downstairs of Gen. Israel Hunt Jr.'s home, which can be seen at the far end of this old photograph of Main Street. During this time, many of Thayer's "new lights" contributed wholesome literature to the newspaper for the mill girls to read as it was a popular publication to the Nashua Manufacturing Company. During the Civil War, this paper became so sympathetic to the south, a large crazed mob of the pro-North majority in town rushed the print house, prepared to tear it down and hang the editor. Hunt, an ardent democrat and owner of the building, took to one of his upper story windows and was able to convince the people to back down from their wrath, especially after he helped convince the editor, B. B. Whittemore, to fulfill their demanding request to display an American Union flag outside for them. (Historic image courtesy FMC.)

This old picture provides a rare view of the original church building on Main Street referred to as the Old Chocolate church. The Nutt building, the first townhouse, and the County Records building are the other prominent structures. A building committee consisting of Israel Hunt Jr., Leonard Noyes, Thomas Chase, Franklin Fletcher, George Y. Sawyer, and Samuel Shepard as architect (proponents for "the south") proposed a lot belonging to Aaron F. Sawyer, who's house can be seen in this old picture next to the first official city hall. Group leaders living north of the river (hence, proponents for "the north") including Daniel Abbot, Charles F. Gove, Charles J. Fox,

William Boardman, and Josiah Graves, were all opposed to any location south of the Nashua River. (Historic image courtesy NPL.)

This is Nashua High School, and its first graduating class, in 1857. This school building on Main Street was first used in 1853, the same year the town became a city. The first high school to be built was while the towns were separated. Under the direction of Daniel Abbot, Nashville built the first high school in 1851. It was built on the site of the current school of Mount Pleasant. In 1869, the high school building on Main Street became the high school for the entire city, the students were educated in this building of approximately 1,500 square feet. In 2005, Nashua's newest high school, Nashua North, educated its first set of "seniors" in the awesome facility of 421,000 square feet, and the teachers are calling it "a dream." (Historic image courtesy NPL.)

Nashua's oldest movie house opened in 1911, the Colonial Theater took over Nashua's first high school building and used its outer walls to house the screen and seats. The main entrance from Main Street brought patrons through an arcade before being able to enter to the shows. For a time during the Depression, the Colonial offered five free tickets weekly to random names pulled from the city directory. People would look in the *Nashua Telegraph* to see if they received a free admission. Other creative marketing schemes were advertised such as grocery give-a-ways, cash jackpots, and children's bicycles. Competition was in effect, so all the theatres of Nashua had some sort of prize to give if you

would attend their theatre. Currently, the merchants called Junz, Myoptic, Damon Real Estate, and Design Wares now line this portion of Main Street. (Historic image courtesy NHS.)

This photograph was taken in 1953 when the Tremont Theatre was known as the Daniel Webster Theatre. The Tremont Theatre opened on May 28, 1917, across the street in the Chase building, then moved to the Merchants Exchange building where it remained open until 1974. The State Theater opened on August 29, 1927, in the Chase building, and always had the best movies; playing films with famous Hollywood types such as Shirley Temple, Bing Crosby, and Katharine Hepburn. The State Theater also conveyed the highest stature of all the theaters of Nashua, and was the place to bring a date to impress them. Martha's Sweet Shop resides in a portion of the space once occupied by the Daniel Webster Theatre. Visible in the "now" photograph are umbrellas the Exchange puts out every warm day for sidewalk-café-style dining. (Historic image courtesy NHS.)

The Park Theater was opened on July 3, 1918, in the 1870 Congregational church building. The Park Theater presented a variety of entertainment; B-films, news, shorts, vaudeville, double features, and "balcony spitballs" were just some of the fun you could obtain for just pennies a seat. It was considerably different from the other theatre's insomuch as its attendees were not always the best in behavior. The downfall of the theaters on Main Street has a logical demise. Television was introduced at the 1939 World's Fair in New York City, and drive-ins had gained immediate popularity upon their arrival in 1933. Residents were moving further into the suburbs and by the late 1970s, the Park Theatre in 1952, the Colonial Theatre

in 1954, the Daniel Webster Theatre in 1974, and the State Theatre in 1976 were all gone. (Historic image courtesy City of Nashua.)

The first train to reach Railroad Square arrived on December 23, 1837. The Concord railroad extension was completed in 1845, and in 1849, Franklin Hall and the passenger station was completed. The second floor of Franklin Hall was used as the Nashville Town Hall for some time. It was also used for Irish services by Fr. John O'Donnell in 1855. Arthur H. Davis reopened the second floor as the Franklin Opera House on February 28, 1890, and it became the most outstanding show theater of southern New Hampshire, attracting many leading actors of the time, such as noted Shakespearean actress Julia Marlowe. Roller-skating, basketball, and wrestling were also enjoyed there as the seats could be removed easily. This building was devastated, on April 19, 1931, by fire. Today the trailer truck has replaced the traveling train, and although the line still exists behind the Dunkin' Donuts, shipments are brought in twice per week by roadway.

This image of Main Street was in the area known as the Harbor. The Harbor name was generated in the early frontier days when American Indian attacks were prevalent. Pioneer families could seek safe harbor in a fortification located in or around the area that is now know as Globe Plaza. Records from 1897 in Parker's "History of the City of Nashua, New Hampshire" say the location was marked, but then lost when a road was created. He also talks about the spot with reference to Miss Allds's house and near where Novelty Works was located. Peter Eddy, a Nashua and New Hampshire photographer, called himself a "view artist," and made this photograph somewhere between 1850

and 1920. The house numbers listed on the homemade albumen real-photo postcard read 294, 296, and 298 Main Street. (Historic image courtesy FMC.)

The Washington House was originally located between High and Factory Streets, on the site of the Noyes building, from 1830 to 1852. Pres. Andrew Jackson had breakfast at the Washington on his way to Concord in 1833. The story is told that

upon Jackson's arrival to Dunstable, he was greeted at the state line with a barouche drawn by six fine white horses. He changed seats from his Lowell transport, and along the way to the Dunstable Common, which was decorated in elaborate greenery for the occasion, he was greeted by an organized pageant of ladies all dressed in white with long ribbon sashes. A large assembly of townspeople was gathered at the top of Indian Head Hill to greet him before he was promenaded back down the street to the Washington House. Thomas Chase was proprietor of the hotel, it was a popular destination for democrats. These photographs show the present location of the removed, famed hotel. (Historic image courtesy NPL.)

The Tremont House was a highly recognized and prized hotel in Nashua for many years. Completed in 1848, its position on Main Street made it a popular congregational site as stagecoaches and later horsecars were always available. At least two United States presidents have made their way to the Tremont House in Nashua. On August 25, 1877, Rutherford B. Hayes attended a banquet there, and later Teddy Roosevelt as a young man made many visits. In 1907, the First National Bank merged with and became the Second National Bank. The Second National Bank acquired the Tremont House in 1922, had the building demolished, and constructed the concrete edifice that was the home to the Bank of New Hampshire for many years before becoming TD Banknorth on May 23, 2005. (Historic image courtesy FMC.)

The first establishment located at this property dates back to 1795 when Thomas French erected a hotel. The Indian Head House was later built upon it in 1801 by Timothy Taylor and had a great share of fame and patronage before it was razed in 1892. In 1894, under the pastoral direction of governor Hugh Gregg's maternal grandfather Cyrus Richardson, the First Church was built there. The October 27, 2004 photograph contains an October "Hunter's Moon" that was also waxing into a rare complete astronomical transient visibility cycle realized periodically when the sun, the moon, and the earth, in that order, come into complete alignment called a total lunar eclipse. During this exceptional celestial event, many in the city were celebrating the Red Sox victory in the World Series. Thomas Weld, said to be the first preacher in Dunstable, was ordained as minister of the First Church Congregation on December 16, 1685. Two total lunar eclipses occurred in 1685, one on June 16 and another on December 10. The next total lunar eclipse visible in Nashua will appear on March 3, 2007. (Historic image courtesy FMC.)